P9-AEV-227

MYSTIC SEAPORT must be seen to be understood and appreciated, so we
are trying here to give you a glimpse, in pictures, of the variety of
this beautiful outdoor museum on the banks of the Mystic River.

IT IS A BIG place of more than forty acres, and a busy, bustling home
for famous ships and small craft, ship models and figureheads, scrimshaw
and paintings. Through craftsmen at work, lecture-demonstrations,
a research library, publications and educational programs, it imparts
a feeling and appreciation of life in nineteenth-century maritime
America to the visitor of today. There is even a shipyard with
a lift dock, for the Seaport is one of the world's few maritime museums
to undertake major preservation of its ships and small craft.

AT MYSTIC SEAPORT the visitor can step back into the past for a moment,
to catch a glimpse of how it used to be in the days of our
forefathers, and to enjoy the beguilements of a seagoing world.

A curve of Seaport Street showing the Bank,
Nantucket Cooperage, the Edwards House, the
Mystic Press and the Hoop Shop

MYSTIC SEAPORT

A MUSEUM DEDICATED TO AMERICA'S MARITIME HERITAGE

PUBLISHED BY

MYSTIC SEAPORT, INC.®

MYSTIC, CONNECTICUT

PHOTOGRAPHERS: Maynard Bray: 41; *Oliver Denison III:*
1, 4, 6, 7, 8, 10, 11, 12, 13, 14, 19, 20, 21, 22, 24,
25, 29, 32, 34, 35, 36, 37, 42, 46, 48; *Sandra DeVeau:* 9;
Russell A. Fowler: 28, 43, 44; *Kenneth Mahler:* 30; *Louis Martel:* 15,
16, 17, 23, 31; *Les Olin:* cover, 12, 18, 26, 38, 39;
Lynn Anderson Peterson: 33; *Mary Anne Stets:* 40, 45,
47; *John F. Urwiller:* 5; *Claire White:* 27

Copyright © 1974 by
Mystic Seaport, Inc.
Library of Congress Catalog
Number: 74-76870
ISBN: 0-913372-11-0

Typeset and printed
by Eastern Press, Inc.
Designed by
Gainor R. Akin
Type is Caledonia

The *Joseph Conrad* dressed for Christmas, seen from across the Mystic River

Seaport reflections of the sandbagger sloop *Annie*,
the cutter *Galena* and the training ship *Joseph Conrad*

A summer band concert on the South Green

The Buckingham House, built in Old Saybrook between
1725 and 1758, and moved to the Seaport in 1951

The Captain's Garden

The *Emma C. Berry*, a Noank smack of 1866 and one
of the oldest commercial sailing vessels in
American documentation, tied up at the dock
in front of the Edwards House

Main shop of the Shipyard, with *Kittiwake* in
foreground, *Annie* by door, *Galena* on the left

The origin of this figurehead called *Asia* is in doubt, but possibly it came from a British naval ship of 1824

Dreaming of days gone by—three goddess-like figureheads in the Stillman Building

Spinning room of the Plymouth Cordage Company
ropewalk, built in 1824 and operated until 1947

Chantey singing had its heyday in the mid-nineteenth
century in the days of the wind ships: the tradition
survives today at the Seaport

The *Brilliant,* a 61-foot auxiliary schooner used as a
training ship by the Seaport's Mariner Programs

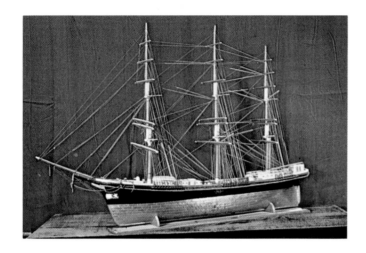

Model of the *Benj. F. Packard*, a 244-foot sailing ship
built in Bath, Maine, in 1883

Bone model of the whaleship *Massachusetts*

Scrimshaw dippers, dust brush and cream pitcher

Photographer's delight: this kitchen window of the Buckingham House

After the rain

Foredeck of the *Charles W. Morgan*

Fore-topsail being bent on the *Conrad*

Dogwood blossoms frame the Pugsley Clock Shop

The double parlor of the Greenman House, built by
Thomas Greenman in 1839

Sandbagger-sloop *Annie*, a champion in her day, was
Mystic-built in 1880. Her sail area is 1,313 square feet.

Steamboat *Sabino*, built at East Boothbay, Maine, in
1908, carries Seaport passengers during the summer months

The Charles Mallory Sail Loft, with the *Conrad* in the background

Conversation piece in the Shipcarver's Shop

Restoration of the Block Island Lifesaving Station

Lobster pots

Caulkers at work on the *Morgan's* hull while on
the lift dock for restoration

The *L.A. Dunton*, a Gloucester fishing schooner, built
by Arthur Story at Essex, Massachusetts, in 1921

The Seaport's colorful fleet of Dyer Dhows
used in its Mariner Training Program

The *Emma C. Berry* is relaunched into the Mystic River
on May 7, 1971, after restoration at the Seaport

In the Ship Chandlery—lanterns, running and anchor lights

In the Rigging Loft—blocks and rigging hardware

Fish plate used to connect the two pieces
of the 92-foot keel assembly from the whaleship
Thames, built in 1818 at Essex, Connecticut

Fishtown Chapel

The annual Christmas Carol Sing in front of the Mallory
Buildings attracts visitors from far and wide

Sailmaker at work in the Charles Mallory Sail Loft.
The potbellied stove is suspended from the ceiling
to give uninterrupted working space.

John Leavitt's painting of the *Charles W. Morgan*
as a double-topsail bark

The Henry B. duPont Preservation Shipyard viewed from the
maintop of the *Morgan* when hauled on the lift dock

New England & The Sea Exhibit

Early morning on Village Street

New York Yacht Club Station #10 displays an extensive
collection of America's Cup memorabilia

The annual Small Craft Workshop crowds the river with small craft of every description. In foreground, an Irish curragh.

Masts and rigging, with the *Morgan* on the
lift dock in the background

A summer demonstration of whaleboat rowing on the Mystic River

New Haven sharpie silhouetted against an evening sky